friendship
isn't a
BIG thing·
it's a
million
little things.

blossom
by blossom
friendship
begins

In the spirit
of FRIENDSHIP
the heart finds
its morning and
is refreshed.

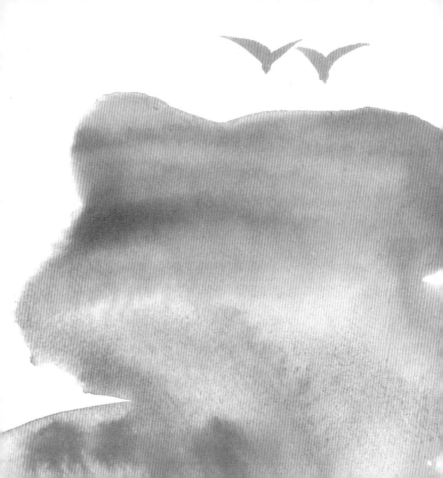

Just
thinking
of
you
makes
me
smile

Where Nature links
A friendly pair
The blessing
is as rich as rare.

SANSKIT

Friendship
is precious
not only in the shade
but in the sunshine
of Life as well.

—THOMAS
JEFFERSON

Friends
have a
wonderful
way of
reminding
us what
really
matters.

Never doubt,
but ONE friend
hears the Music
of your soul.

WANG WEI

An acquaintance
is someone
we can say Hello to;
a Friend
is someone
we can say
anything to.

When I hear
your voice
it is a song
that comforts
my spirit.

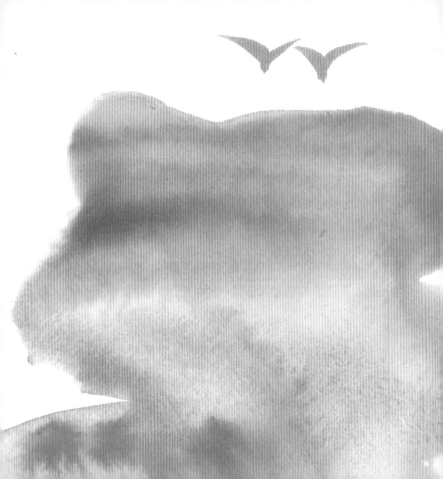

We each have our sorrows to bear;
we each have our gifts to share.

when I choose a friend,
I choose one who loves truth,
respects Life and me,
one who hears music
and sees the moon,
one who loves to see me smiling.

I always
wanted
to have
a friend
like you.

A trusted friend is one
of Life's greatest treasures.

Can you ever know
what a joy it is
to have you
in my Life ?

Friendship
is a gift
you give
all year;
the growth
of friendship
a lifetime
affair.

—AARON LOCKS

We grow like Great Flowers
in the Light
of our own Truth
and Friendship.

I love the variety
of our friendship
The flowing freedom
of ourselves to
be ourselves.

I love the way
we argue -
we both come
out winning -
you
for us!

Don't walk in front of me.
I may not follow.
Don't walk behind me.
I may not lead.
Just walk beside me
And be my Friend.

- ALBERT CAMUS

Its better to walk with a friend.

FROM BERLINPLATZ

may
the
hand
of a
FRIEND
always
be
near
you.

- IRISH BLESSING

If you're
a little
BOAT
with
nowhere
to go,
just tell me
where
you're tied
and I'll
row out
to meet you.

/ BOOK OF GENJI

How precious are the gifts of myself
to you. How precious are the
gifts of yourself to me.

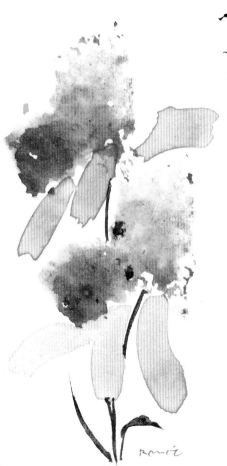

You are a
DELICIOUS
experience

I see you and know the world is beautiful

My friend, how wonderful it is to say you are MY FRIEND.

· JAMES GATES

As Spring sings
   eternal,
your Life shall never
   lack a Friend.